CLAUDE MICHEL

BIRDS

OF

MAURITIUS

New Edition

EDITIONS DE L'OCEAN INDIEN

© Claude Michel
Editions de l'Océan Indien (1992)

Photographs : Nick Garbutt
               Colin Taylor

Cover   : Nick Garbutt

Illustrations : Wahab Owadally
                Nazli Foondun

Published by :

Editions de l'Océan Indien
Stanley, Rose-Hill
Mauritius

Typesetting :

Mauritius Printing Specialists (Pte) Ltd (1992)
Stanley, Rose-Hill
Mauritius

Printing :

Kin Keong Printing Co. Pte Ltd (1992)
2nd reprint: Kin Keong Printing Co. Pte Ltd (1998)
3rd reprint: King Keong Printing Co. Pte Ltd (2000)
Reprint: Markono Print Media Pte Ltd (2003)

1st Edition **MIE – (1981)**
2nd Edition **EOI – (1986)**
3rd Edition **EOI – (1992)**

ISBN 99903-0-140-9

FOREWORD

This booklet was first published by the Mauritius Institute of Education in 1981 to help secondary school teachers and pupils interested in wild animals. The information was mainly obtained from the available literature.

In 1986 the Editions de l'Océan Indien published an illustrated version and for that edition my thanks are due to Carl Jones (Conservation Field Officer, Jersey Wildlife Preservation Trust) and Wahab Owadally (Conservator of Forests) for pointing out various errors in the first edition. They also kindly looked through the manuscript of the second edition.

A few more notes on some endemic birds supplement this third edition and the coloured illustrations have been changed. My thanks are due to Nick Garbutt for providing a number of papers, including his unpublished reports on the Kestrel, from which the added notes have been derived.

For the drawings I wish to thank Wahab Owadally and Mrs Nazli Foondun and for the photographs Nick Garbutt and Colin Taylor.

The scientific names used are in accordance with Howard and Ward's Complete Checklist of the Birds of the World, O.U.P. 1980.

C.M.

INTRODUCTION

A. Previous work done

The first record of bird life here is the impression left on the Dutch, who first visited the island, by the abundance of the avifauna. These visitors list turtle-doves, herons, parrots, owls, swallows as well as wild geese and dwell long on the massacres perpetrated. Captive parrots for example were persuaded to call so as to attract their kind which were slaughtered. The Dutch also mention in their accounts the dodo, a bird which became extinct during the first occupation of our island.

Another record prepared during the Dutch period was that of a Frenchman, François Leguat, who was long held prisoner and lived on tiny Ile aux Vacoas, after some problems with the authorities on ambergris. The most interesting feature of his account is mention of a bird, since referred to as Leguat's giant, which appears to belong more to fiction than fact as no bone of this "giant" has been found so far. Some scientists think that Leguat's "giant" may have been a flamingo, a species which visited our island in the past.

Birds of many feathers flocked together in Bernardin de Saint-Pierre's "Voyage à l'Ile de France" published during the French period. The account is more poetic than scientific but science came into its own with Commerson, a French naturalist who stayed long — and died — on our island. Drawings of plants and animals were executed by another Frenchman, Jossigny, under Commerson's supervision, but most of Commerson's work has not appeared in print with the exception of some notes used by Buffon in his great work.

The 19th century saw more mention of birds in Milbert's "Voyage pittoresque à l'Ile de France" as well as in Colonel Pike's "Sub-

tropical rambles in the land of the Aphanapteryx". This Aphanapteryx was a bird, now extinct. The colonel's book brims with that victorian charm which has today yielded to the dry and impersonal — if scientific — account. The author seems to have been as interested in natural history as in his work, which was that of American consul here.

More formal accounts of birds were published in the 19th century first by an English ornithologist, Edward Newton, while the most comprehensive set of observations was signed by a Frenchman, Oustalet, near the end of the century. It is unfortunate that the observations of a dynamic Mauritian naturalist, Julien Desjardins, whose collections started our natural history museum, were not printed. Few traces of his work have reached us.

Many papers, as shown by the list at the end of these notes, have appeared during the 20th century. Guérin, a Mauritian ornithologist, has recorded not only the bibliography of previous work done but has also summarised the information available on the morphology and behaviour of our birds. It is regrettable that the work was limited to 30 copies.

A scientific mission coming from abroad has recently studied our bird fauna. The result of the work has appeared in 1987 under the editorship of A. W. Diamond. The scientists concerned have added to visual observations recordings of songs and calls, so as to be able to analyse behaviour more competently. The local authorities have not been indifferent to the fate of our birds and laws exist protecting them, forbidding killing, capture, sale, etc., of birds with the exception of a few species considered pests or game birds.

Pictorial representations of our birds include photographs in the works listed below; drawings by Jean Michel Vinson published in Le Cernéen; a set of small coloured cards published by the Mauritius Commercial Bank; a calendar sponsored by the State Commercial Bank; postcards published by the Mauritius Institute; posters, particularly of the Kestrel and the Pink Pigeon, and several sets of postage stamps. Drawings as well as a record of calls of a number of birds can be found in the guide to the Sir Seewoosagur Ramgoolam Botanic Garden published by the Conservator of Forests, Mr W. Owadally.

We should not, it is true, speak ill of the dead. But one can speak too well of them. Such has been the case of a story concocted by a visiting ornithologist on the relationship existing between a native plant, the **tambalacoque (Sideroxylon grandiflorum)** *and the dodo. The gradual disappearance of the tree was attributed to the disappearance of the dodo which, supposedly, ate its fruits and rejected the seeds. Their passage through the alimentary canal of the bird was said to have been essential for germination.*

The story is such a pretty one, and, if true, would have been such an ecological gem, that it is oft quoted as an example of balance in Nature. Unfortunately it happens to be untrue for several reasons. The bird and the tree did not share the same habitat. Moreover seeds of **tambalacoque** *have been germinated without the help of any bird, and some young* **tambalacoque,** *less than a century old, exist in the native forests.*

Man's arrival on the island initiated a series of changes which were to prove catastrophic for the native wildlife. As a start felling of trees for various purposes deprived the birds of food, cover and nesting sites. By 1880 there remained less than 4 per cent of the virgin forest which once covered Mauritius. During the 20th century forest destruction continued, to obtain land for tea and pine plantations. The havoc has been fortunately halted in the 1980's.

Animals, deliberately or accidentally introduced, have added their misdeeds to the misfortunes of the avifauna. They still contribute to the decline of the native bird population. The early comers were monkeys, rats, feral pigs and deer which were joined later by feral cats. In the early 1900's mongooses were brought in to control rats. The harm done by animals lies partly in the competition for food, for example monkeys and rats eat plant parts of use to birds. In addition monkeys and rats raid nests while rats and others, even bees, compete for nest holes. Ground living animals such as the deer and pig trample vegetation while feral cats and mongooses attack young kestrels and pigeons which spend some time on the ground. A non living plague, the cyclone, from time to time adds its quota of destruction to the seasonal shortage of food. Under the burden of calamities some species such as the kestrel would have disappeared were it not for conservation measures carried out with considerable help from foreign organisations. The eventual aim is to release in the wild birds bred in captivity. It seems that current efforts will enable the establishment of stable populations of two species, the kestrel and the pink pigeon.

Some works dealing with our birds:

DIAMOND, E.W. (ed.) 1987: **Studies of Mascarene island birds.**

GUERIN, R. 1940 — 1952. **Faune ornithologique ancienne et actuelle des Iles Mascareignes.**

JONES, Carl G. and OWADALLY, A. W. 1988: The life histories and conservation of the Mauritius kestrel **Falco punctatus,** pink pigeon, **Columba mayeri,** and echo parakeet, **Psittacula eques. Proceedings of the Royal Society of Arts and Sciences of Mauritius** vol.5 pt. 1.

JONES, Carl G. and ors. A summary of the conservation management of the Mauritius kestrel **Falco punctatus** 1973-1991; **Dodo. Jersey wildlife Preservation Trust** vol. 27.

Mc KELVY, D. S. 1976: A preliminary study of the Mauritian Pink Pigeon. **Mauritius Institute Bulletin; vol. 8, pt 2.**

MEINHERTZHAGEN, R. 1912: On the birds of Mauritius; **Ibis.**

NEWTON, E. 1861: Ornithological notes from Mauritius; **Ibis.**

NEWTON, R. Ornithological notes on Mauritius and the Cargados Carajos Archipelago: **Proceedings of the Royal Society of Arts and Sciences of Mauritius;** vol. 2 pt.1.

OUSTALET, E. 1896-1897: Notice sur la faune ornithologique ancienne et moderne des Iles Mascareignes et en particulier de l'Ile Maurice: **Annales des Sciences Naturelles, Zoologie.**

ROUNTREE, F. R. G. 1951: Some aspects of bird life in Mauritius; **Proceedings of the Royal Society of Arts and Sciences of Mauritius** vol.1 pt. 2.

ROUNTREE F. R. G. and ors. 1952: Catalogue of the birds of Mauritius; **Mauritius Institute Bulletin** vol. 3 pt. 3.

SAFFORD, Roger, J. 1991: Status and ecology of the Mauritius fody **Foudia rubra** and Mauritius olive white-eye **Zosterops chloronothos:** two Mauritian passerines in danger. **Dodo, Jersey Wildlife Preservation Trust** vol. 27.

STAUB, F. 1973: **Oiseaux de l'Ile Maurice et de Rodrigues.**

STAUB, F. 1976: **Birds of the Mascarenes and Saint Brandon.**

*STAUB, F. 1988: Evolutionary trends in some Mauritian phanerogams in relation to their pollinators; **Proceedings of the Royal Society of Arts and Sciences of Mauritius** vol. 5 pt.1. STORER and ors, 1963 **Preliminary field guide to the birds of the Indian Ocean.***

B. State of the Fauna

Our bird fauna has various origins. The most interesting component is the endemic, i.e. those species produced in Mauritius itself by evolution and therefore not found outside our island. The oldest rocks here are some 7 million years old and though volcanic eruptions following their formation have produced the majority of the rocks (and the derived soils) which we see today, the eruptions did not all occur at the same time and may have left islands of soil and rock where life could continue.

We do not know the nature and number of the first birds, which came to the new island, saw, conquered a place to live — and evolved into new species. Fossil remains tell us that the past fauna was much richer than it is today. Some birds may have disappeared through natural causes but many became extinct recently through man's activities: destruction of native forests, and introduction of animals which compete with birds or attack them. Out of the nine endemics now left, only one, the grey white eye (pic pic) by adapting itself to man made habitats, is common all over the island.

The second component of the fauna, the indigenous, is not much in evidence. Indigenous birds are those which came here under their own power and are found in other countries as well as our own. The group includes oceanic birds nesting on Round and Serpent Islands. The most interesting species in the group is the Trinidade Petrel which, apart from Round Island, nests in only one other part of the world, Trinidade (off Brazil). It is possible that its distribution was much more extensive in the past but has been reduced by various causes. Our marine birds have sorted themselves out into two groups: one, the tropic birds, the petrel and the shearwater nesting on Round Island; the other comprising terns, and a booby keeping to Serpent Island.

Oceanic birds are conspicuous not only because they have webbed feet but also because the young are covered with fluff and only later acquire adult plumage. They go far out to sea to obtain food — which is sometimes contaminated by DDT as seen in the eggs of the petrel.

The third component, the exotic, consists of the birds introduced deliberately or accidentally by man. The distinction between exotic (introduced) and indigenous birds does not seem very important and in the case of two birds, the wild duck and the moorhen, there is no evidence to enable one to tell whether they came here by themselves or were introduced by man. The exotic birds are the common birds of town or country — pic-pic excepted.

The final component consists of the migrating species of which many come regularly to Mauritius during our summer, while others have only rarely been observed. The remarkable feature of migration is the ability of the bird to find tiny Mauritius in the wide Indian Ocean. Scientists think that migrating birds navigate with the help of the stars. One of the most impressive of these migrants is the turnstone, a tiny creature which nests as far North as latitude 80 degrees, though we cannot know whether all turnstones coming to Mauritius travel that far.

Whether exotic or endemic, birds form a fascinating group. They can be studied for pleasure as well as for filling gaps in our knowledge. Among the topics generally studied are observations associated with nesting (sex of nest builder; parent sitting on the eggs; height and type of nest; number and shape of eggs; time taken to hatch; time taken for young to leave the nest; nest hygiene, lining of nest). Courtship, display and territorial or general behaviour, distribution according to vegetation and altitude form another aspect of study, while morphology and variations according to age, sex or season must not be neglected. For example various species like the mynah, pic-pic and bulbul show complete or partial albinism, while the bright red of the male cardinal is replaced, in some individuals, by yellow feathers.

A nature diary is essential if observations are to be followed, and keeping one ultimately proves rewarding.

BIRD LIST

A

ENDEMICS

1. **Blackbird** *(Plate 1)*
   Merle
   Hypsipetes olivaceus

HABITAT : Various native forests, e.g. Bel Ombre, Savanne, Bambous, Black River.

FOOD : Omnivore. Eats fruits, insects, even small lizards.

REPRODUCTION : Two pinkish-white, spotted eggs laid in a rather untidy, cup-shaped nest made of fairly thick plant parts like grass leaves. Nest placed in vegetation a few metres above ground level. Both male and female sit on the eggs. Incubation time 15 days. Young stay a further 3 weeks in nest.

REMARKS : The bird often travels in small groups. Male and female plumage alike. Yellow bill of both sexes conspicuous. Voice pleasant.
   Quick to sound the alert when disturbed.
   Illustrated on a former 50 cent stamp and a calendar published by the State Commercial Bank.*

Order Passeriformes.   *Fam. Pycnonotidae.*

---

*Besides the illustrations mentioned for this and the other species, photographs appear in the books and papers mentioned in the list of works quoted.

2.   Cuckoo-shrike *(Plate 2)*
Cuisinier; Pie-grièche
Coracina typica

HABITAT : Remnants of native forests round Black River Gorges; Bel Ombre forest.

FOOD : Insects hunted for in vegetation. Occasionally robs nests of other birds like the Pink Pigeon, sucking the eggs.

REPRODUCTION : Two to three pale-green spotted eggs laid in a rough, cup-shaped nest of thin plant parts bound by cobwebs and placed high in trees. Both parents sit on the eggs. Nest predated by rats.

REMARKS : The sexes are different, the female being russet-brown, the male basically grey. Not common but numbers have seemed stable for some time around 200 pairs. Illustrated on a postcard and a former 20 cent stamp.

Order Passeriformes.   Fam. Campephagidae.

3. Echo parakeet *(Plate 3)*
Grosse cato verte
Psittacula eques

HABITAT : Formerly existed wherever there was forest.

FOOD : Prefers fruits but takes seeds, leaves, flowers and occasionally bark of some trees.

REPRODUCTION : 2-4 eggs laid in holes of trees. There is a strong pair bond. The female sits on the eggs and is fed by the male. Incubation about three weeks. The young stay in the nest till 50 days old.

REMARKS : The male is distinguished from the female by a black and pink collar. In addition the male beak is pink and the female's grey. Must not be confused with the introduced parrot which is smaller and whose female has a red beak.
The parakeet was still common in the 1830's. Declined by the late 19th century and continued to fall during our times. In 1991 only some 15 birds were known in the wild.

Order Psittaciformes. *Fam. Psittacidae.*

4. Fly catcher *(Plate 4)*
Coq des bois; Gobe mouches
Terpsiphone bourbonnensis

HABITAT   : Scattered vegetation in very patchy distribution. Numbers continue to decline.

FOOD   : Insects caught on the wing.

REPRODUCTION : About three spotted eggs laid in a carefully made, cup-shaped nest of thin plant parts held by cobwebs. Nest placed in dense vegetation some 3 metres above ground. Male and female sit on the eggs. Hatching time some 12 days. Young stay a further fortnight in the nest.

REMARKS   : Male head iridescent dark blue with a large crest. Female head greyish blue with smaller crest. Bird very familiar, tame and inquisitive. Lovely song. Illustrated on a former 5 cent stamp and a calendar published by the State Commercial Bank.

Order Passeriformes.   *Fam. Muscicapidae.*

5. Grey white eye *(Plate 5)*
Pic-pic; Zozo manioc; Oiseau blanc
Zosterops borbonica

HABITAT   : Common all over the island.

FOOD   : Basically insects picked off plants or occasionally caught in flight. Also takes nectar from some flowers.

REPRODUCTION : Two to three pale blue eggs laid in a delicate nest of thin plant material.

REMARKS   : This is the only endemic bird to have adapted itself to man-made conditions. Gregarious and moves in bands of 6 to 20 throughout the year. Male and female plumage identical.
White rump conspicuous, body grey.
Illustrated on a former 2 cent stamp.

Order Passeriformes.   *Fam. Zosteropidae.*

Blackbird

Colin Taylor

PLATE 1

Colin Taylor   *Cuckooshrike*

PLATE 2

Nick Garbutt   *Young echo Parakeet*

PLATE 3

Colin Taylor

Fly Catcher

PLATE 4

Nick Garbutt

Mauritius Fody

Colin Taylor

Grey white eye

PLATE 5

Nick Garbutt

Kestrel

PLATE 6

Colin Taylor   *Olive white eye*

PLATE 7

Nick Garbutt

Pink Pigeon

PLATE 8

6. Kestrel *(Plate 6)*
Crécerelle
Falco punctatus

FOOD   : Eats mainly brightly coloured Phelsuma lizards which it stalks by flying from tree to tree. Also takes insects like grasshoppers or dragonflies, small birds and occasionally shrews.

REPRODUCTION : Two to four white spotted eggs in holes of trees or cliffs. They hatch in about 4 weeks and the young leave the nest when about 5 weeks old. The male feeds the young when they are still small. Later the female may help in food catching. Breeding success is poor since all pairs do not reproduce every year and a pair succeeds in producing only one young per year. Inbreeding may have been a contributing factor to the decline.

REMARKS   : As in all birds of prey the head can rotate far back. Male and female plumage identical but the adult male is slightly smaller than the female.
The bird is thought to have existed all over the island. Bernardin de Saint Pierre, the author of *Paul et Virginie* who visited us in 1768 even records kestrels at the seaside. By the late nineteenth century however numbers had been seriously reduced. The mistaken accusation that the bird ate poultry led to its name *mangeur de poules* and did not endear it to the population. Decline paralleled the dwindling forests, land being cleared for cultivation. A further bane during the 20th century was added to the reduction of the forest area: the use of organochloride pesticides. In 1974 the population reached a bottom low of 6 individuals.

A conservation campaign started in 1973 with attempts at rearing the bird in captivity. In spite of intensive efforts there were more downs than ups in the programme and by 1980 the captive birds had died. A fresh start was made in 1981 and under the leadership of Carl Jones of the Jersey Wildlife Preservation Trust, captive breeding has met with success. Kestrels have not simply been reared in Mauritius but also abroad.

Release in the wild is carefully arranged. Birds about thirty days old are placed in nest holes, fed with white mice and watched over till they do not need human support. Nest boxes are provided in the hope that they will be used by breeding pairs but mynahs also find them suitable. Field biologists spend much time surveying the released birds and have noted successful nesting.

Illustrated on a postcard, a former 25 cent stamp, a stamp issue in 1984 and a number of photographs and posters.

Order Falconiformes.   *Fam. Falconidae.*

7.   **Mauritius fody** *(Plate 5)*
      Cardinal de Maurice; Oiseau banane
      Foudia rubra

HABITAT   : Formerly common. It is thought that reference by
                    early Dutch settlers to sparrows may have related
                    to cardinal birds. Now reduced to a very small
                    area of native forest.

FOOD   : Basically insects but also takes odd fruit and
                    nectar. Noticed probing wood or epiphytic mosses
                    for insects.

REPRODUCTION :   Three pale blue eggs laid in a rough, dome-shaped
                    nest of plant parts e.g. grasses, roots, moss. Nest
                    preferably placed well above ground in tree tops
                    but predated by introduced animals. Territorial.

REMARKS   : The male has a bright red head and throat. This
                    colour disappears during the non-breeding season.
                    The population estimated in 1975 at 250 pairs had
                    declined to an estimated 90 pairs in 1990. The
                    madagascar fody on losing the breeding plumage
                    has on occasion been confused with the Mauritian
                    one.
                    Figured on a postcard and a former 10 cent stamp.

                    Order Passeriformes.   *Fam. Ploceidae.*

8. Olive white eye *(Plate 7)*
Oiseau à lunettes; Yeux blancs
Zosterops chloronothos

HABITAT   : Remnants of native vegetation of higher altitudes.

FOOD   : Basically nectar of various flowers including introduced ones like the bottlebrush. Also picks off insects from vegetation.

REPRODUCTION : Two pale eggs in a delicate, cup-shaped nest of thin plant material well hidden in foliage. Incubation about two weeks. The birds cover a wide range in the non-breeding period.

REMARKS   : Conspicuous white circle round eye. Male and female plumage alike. Numbers have sadly declined from an estimated 300 pairs in 1975 to about half that number in 1990.
Illustrated on a former 4 cent stamp and a calendar published by the State Commercial Bank.

Order Passeriformes.   *Fam. Zosteropidae.*

9. Pink pigeon *(Plate 8)*
Pigeon des mares; Pigeon rose
Columba mayeri

FOOD : Feeds upon buds, leaves, flowers, fruits and seeds of a variety of native and introduced plants e.g. *vieille fille* (Lantana). It will take fallen seeds or fruits on the ground.

REPRODUCTION : One or two white eggs laid on a rough platform made by the female from twigs brought by the male. He also marks out a territory around the chosen tree and chases out intruders. Both sexes sit on the eggs, the female being on night duty from late afternoon to early morning, the male incubating during day time. Incubation lasts about 2 weeks, and as in other pigeons, the young are fed with regurgitated food called crop milk. Vegetable matter, such as leaves and seeds, is added after the first four days and gradually increased. The young leave the nest when about 3 weeks old. Breeding success is low, only some 10 per cent.

REMARKS : Male and female plumage identical. The birds have been reported to be sometimes drowsy after eating berries of *Stillingia*.
The pink pigeon very likely lived all over the island. Early Dutch settlers killed pigeons near the coast and record that they were very tame. Decline was not long to follow and in the 19th century the bird was restricted to forest areas in the uplands and considered rare by the turn of the century. In the 1950's the population was reduced to some 50 birds falling to about twenty in 1986 in a small area some 25 square kilometres in the south west.

A captive breeding programme started in 1976. The bird has been successfully bred locally and abroad, mainly at the Jersey Wildlife Preservation Trust. Release was attempted in 1984 in the Sir Seewoosagur Botanic Garden, Pamplemousses. It failed mainly due to killing by man. A lonely pair survived a couple of years. Undeterred by this misfortune the responsible personnel is releasing pigeons in two areas of the forest, one of which the remaining wild stock occupies.

Illustrated on a post card, a former 35 cent stamp and a set of four stamps in 1985.

Order Columbiformes.   *Fam. Columbidae.*

B

INDIGENOUS

(i) OCEANIC SPECIES

1. Blue faced booby
   Fou
   Sula dactylatra

HABITAT : Serpent Island.

FOOD : Marine animals, e.g. flying fishes.

REPRODUCTION : One egg laid without nest. (Two eggs sometimes laid but only one taken care of).

REMARKS : Not abundant. Male and female alike. Plumage of young different from that of adult.

Order Pelecaniformes.   *Fam. Sulidae.*

2.   Brown noddy *(Plate 9)*
   Macoua
   Anoüs stolidus

HABITAT   : Serpent Island.

FOOD   : Marine animals, e.g. fish, crustacea, molluscs.

REPRODUCTION : One spotted egg. Rough nest placed in vegetation by lesser noddy but may be on ground in the case of the brown noddy. Male and female sit on egg.

REMARKS   : Male and female plumage similar. Both noddies look very much alike but can be told apart when specimens are compared. Name Macoua (black) refers to people of the Macoua tribe.

Order Charadriiformes.   *Fam. Laridae.*

3.   Lesser noddy
   Marianne
   Anoüs tenuirostris

Brown Noddies

PLATE 9

Indigenous

Red-tailed Tropic Bird

Nick Garbutt

PLATE 10

Trinidade Petrel on nest

Nick Garbutt

PLATE 11

Indigenous

White-tailed Tropic Bird with young

Nick Garbutt

PLATE 12

4.   Red-tailed tropic bird*(Plate 10)*
Paille-en-queue à brins rouges
Phaethon rubricauda

HABITAT : Round Island, Gunners Coin. In addition the white tailed tropic bird is seen on the mainland and nests in some river gorges.

FOOD : Marine animals, e.g. squid and flying fish.

REPRODUCTION : One pinkish, spotted egg laid without a nest in some cavity or protected point. Both male and female sit on egg.

REMARKS : Plumage of young different from that of adult. In the case of the white-tailed tropic bird there are two long white feathers in the tail, these feathers being red in the red-tailed bird. The latter is also larger and has a pink sheen to its white feathers. Ringing experiments have shown that the red tailed birds found on Round Island migrate far away. Tropic birds passing far overhead cause children to rub their nails saying: *"Pay an ké, pay an ké, do moa enn ti paké poson"*.

Order Pelecaniformes.   Fam. Phaethontidae.

5. Sooty tern
Yéyé
Sterna fuscata

HABITAT   : Serpent Island.

FOOD   : Marine animals.

REPRODUCTION : One spotted egg laid without a nest. Eggs laid close together.

REMARKS   : Juvenile sooty tern has a plumage different from that of the parents.

Order Charadriiformes.   *Fam. Laridae.*

6. Trinidade petrel *(Plate 11)*
Pétrel de la Trinité
Pterodroma arminjoniana

HABITAT   : Round Island.

FOOD   : Marine animals.

REPRODUCTION : One large, white, unspotted egg laid without a nest in a crevice or beneath some overhanging rock. Both male and female sit on egg. Young leaves nest after some two and a half months.

REMARKS   : This bird has a very restricted distribution and is known to nest in only one other part of the world apart from Round Island, Trinidade, off Brazil.

Order Procellariiformes.   *Fam. Procellariidae.*

7. Wedged-tailed shearwater
Fouquet
Puffinus pacificus

HABITAT   : Round Island.

FOOD   : Marine animals.

REPRODUCTION : Single white egg laid in a burrow dug by the bird.
                    Both male and female sit on the egg.

REMARKS   : Bites fiercely any intruder interfering with its nest.
                    Has a mournful call which alarms superstitious
                    people. Fairly abundant. Male and female alike.

Order Procellariiformes.   Fam. Procellariidae.

8. White-tailed tropic bird *(Plate 12)*
Paille-en-queue à brins blancs
Phaethon lepturus *(see page 15)*

(ii) LAND OR MARSH

1.   Cave swiflet
Petite hirondelle; Salangane
Collocalia francica

HABITAT   : Generally found close to caves in which it nests. Disturbance of caves has recently resulted in a decline of the population.

FOOD   : Insects caught on the wing.

REPRODUCTION : Some three white eggs laid in a small nest of specially secreted saliva mixed with plant parts like lichens, thin grasses. Nest stuck to walls of caves.

REMARKS   : Distinctive white rump seen in flight. Peculiar flutter of wings in flight. Is not a swallow but a martinet. Detects objects by a sonar system. Is at the origin of the line *"Zirondel banbou pran la pli do moa soley"*.

Order Apodiformes.   *Fam. Apodidae.*

2. Little green heron
Gasse
Butorides striatus

HABITAT   : Near fresh or brackish water.

FOOD   : Freshwater animals, e.g. fish, frogs, shrimps,
                   crabs.

REPRODUCTION : Two to four pale-blue eggs laid in a rough nest of
                   twigs, well hidden and often placed in mangrove
                   above water. Occasionally a number of birds nest
                   close together. Incubation time 21-25 days. Young
                   leave nest a fortnight later.

REMARKS   : Fairly common. Solitary. Moves easily on mud.
                   Male and female plumage similar. Stays for hours
                   on end, perched on a branch waiting for food.
                   Sometimes called *crabier* due to habit of eating
                   crustacea.

Order Ciconiiformes.   *Fam. Ardeidae.*

3.   Madagascar turtle-dove
Pigeon ramier
Streptopelia picturata

HABITAT   : Well wooded areas.

FOOD   : Small berries, seeds.

REPRODUCTION : Two white eggs laid in a rough nest of plant parts placed in vegetation some four to ten metres above ground. Incubation period about 15 days. Young leave nest about a fortnight later.

REMARKS   : Name *ramier* derived from *rameau* due to bird living in trees. Male and female plumage alike. Considered by some authors to be an exotic (introduced) species.

Order Columbiformes.   *Fam. Columbidae.*

4. Mascarene martin
    Grosse hirondelle
    Phedina borbonica

HABITAT   : Found near the coast, particularly the southern
                   coast.

FOOD   : Insects caught on the wing.

REPRODUCTION : Some three, white, spotted eggs laid in a large nest
                of thin plant material. Aquatic material sometimes
                included. Nest placed in cracks, etc. of boulders or
                other similar shelter. Known to nest close to man-
                made structures. Only female sits on the eggs but
                male helps to feed the young.

REMARKS   : Male and female plumage alike. Is a true swallow.

                   Order Passeriformes.   *Fam. Hirundinidae.*

C

EXOTIC (Introduced)

1. Barred ground dove; Zebra dove
Petite tourterelle
Geopelia striata

HABITAT : Common in open places where it is seen feeding on the ground.

FOOD : Seeds of various plants.

REPRODUCTION : Two white eggs laid in a perfunctory nest of twigs. Nest fairly low in vegetation. Hatching time about fifteen days. Young stay about 12 days more in nest.

REMARKS : Introduced in French times from the Malaysian area. Male and female colour alike. Generally seen in groups feeding on the ground, sometimes with the spotted dove.

Order Columbiformes.   *Fam. Columbidae.*

2.   House sparrow
Moineau
Passer domesticus

HABITAT : Common all over the island, near human habitations.

FOOD : Omnivore: Feeds on fruits, seeds, insects, household scraps.

REPRODUCTION : Five to six eggs laid in a rough nest which is covered if placed in unsheltered places. Location variable, trees and buildings being used indifferently.
Couples sometimes mate long before actual egg laying.

REMARKS : Introduced from India *ca* 1860. Male and female very different in colouration. Species indulges in occasional dust baths. Many individuals gather noisily in some favourite trees for communal roosting at a time slightly different from that of the mynah.

Order Passeriformes.   *Fam. Ploceidae.*

3. Indian grey francolin
Perdrix
Francolinus pondicerianus

HABITAT   : Occasional in open country.

FOOD   : Various seeds. Rarely insects.

REPRODUCTION : Eight to twelve nearly white eggs laid in a nest on the ground. Incubation time 23 days.

REMARKS   : Introduced from India in French times. Male and female alike. Was formerly abundant but has been decimated by the mongoose introduced in the early 1900's. Lives in groups of four to eight or more.

Order Galliformes.   *Fam. Phasianidae.*

4. Indian house crow *(Illus. on page 26)*
Corbeau de l'Inde
Corvus splendens

HABITAT   : Plaine Verte area in Port Louis but is now spreading.

FOOD   : Omnivore, feeds on various things including carrion and household refuse.

REPRODUCTION : Four blue-green, spotted eggs in a rough nest of twigs placed in trees. A few breeding pairs choose the same tree.

REMARKS   : This species has been introduced here at various times. The present population is probably a recent introduction of the end of the 1960's.

Order Passeriformes.   *Fam. Corvidae.*

Indian house Crow

Madagascar Moorhen

5. King reed hen; Purple swamp hen
Poule sultane
Porphyrio madagascariensis

HABITAT   : Occasional in some marshy areas.

FOOD   : Aquatic vegetation or animals.

REPRODUCTION :   Three to five yellowish, spotted eggs laid in a rough nest well hidden in reeds.

REMARKS   : Does not often fly. Attacks nests of other birds. Male and female alike. Introduced in French times and now extremely rare. One specimen seen at Flic-en-Flac in 1976.

Order Gruiformes.   *Fam. Rallidae.*

6. Madagascar moorhen *(Illus. on page 26)*
Poule d'eau
Gallinula chloropus

HABITAT   : Freshwater bodies like slow flowing rivers or ponds where there is good cover.

FOOD   : Seeds and other parts of aquatic plants, small aquatic animals like shrimps or snails.

REPRODUCTION :   Five to six white, spotted eggs laid in a nest well hidden in reeds above water.

REMARKS   : Probably introduced in French times. Thought by some authors to be indigenous. Swims easily on the water and quickly retires to cover when alarmed.

Order Gruiformes.   *Fam. Rallidae.*

7. Madagascar red fody *(Plate 13)*
Cardinal de Madagascar
Foudia madagascariensis

HABITAT   : Occasional all over the island.

FOOD   : Small seeds, grains, etc., e.g. those of grasses.

REPRODUCTION : Three to four pale-blue eggs laid in a rough nest with lateral opening some 2 metres above ground level. Nest sometimes overhanging water. Female only builds nest, male staying in attendance and displaying nearby.

REMARKS   : Introduced during the French period. Nests of some breeding couples occasionally in close proximity, but male normally defends a territory. Male plumage bright red during the breeding season. The male breeding plumage is yellow in some individuals. The birds flock with waxbills and spice finches to feed on Panicum and the like in the non-breeding season. Known to flock even in the breeding season. Must not be confused with the Mauritius fody in which the male has a much smaller red area.

Order Passeriformes.   *Fam. Ploceidae.*

8.   Meller's duck
Canard sauvage
Anas melleri

HABITAT   : Areas close to freshwater.

FOOD   : Leaves, seeds, etc. of aquatic plants as well as matter sifted from mud.

REPRODUCTION : Eight to sixteen yellowish-white eggs laid in a nest of dead grass and rushes placed on land close to water. Incubation period about 4 weeks. Young stay one day in nest. Only female sits on eggs.

REMARKS   : Sexes alike but male plumage more brilliant during the reproductive season. Webbed feet enable the bird to swim easily on the water surface. Now rare but efforts are being made to save the species by a local enthusiast, as well as the Jersey Wildlife Preservation Trust.

Order Anseriformes.   *Fam. Anatidae.*

NOTE   : A few years ago, the Mallard, *Anas platyrhynchos* (French *Colvert*) has been released near Tamarind Falls and can occasionally be seen in the area.

9. Mynah *(Plate 14)*
Martin
Acridotheres tristis

HABITAT : Common all over the island.

FOOD : Omnivore: eats fruits, insects and occasionally seeds.

REPRODUCTION : Four to five blue-green eggs in a rough nest placed in holes of trees, etc. Material for nest consists of plant parts but may include rags, paper, etc. Both parents sit on the eggs.

REMARKS : Many birds congregate noisily in some favourite tree at nightfall for communal roosting. Noisy period different from that of the sparrow which has the same habit. Sometimes seen on deer and cattle from which the birds pick off ticks. Very aggressive towards the young of other birds. Was introduced in the 1760's to control locusts. Can be trained to talk. Walks instead of hopping. Yellow bill and legs.

Order Passeriformes.   *Fam. Sturnidae.*

Exotic

Nick Garbutt

Ring-necked Parakeet

Nick Garbutt

Madagascar Fody

PLATE 13

Nick Garbutt

Mynah

PLATE 14

Colin Taylor

Waxbill

Colin Taylor

Red whiskered Bulbul

PLATE 15

Nick Garbutt

Village Weaver

PLATE 16

10. Red whiskered bulbul; Persian nightingale *(Plate 15)*
Boulboul; Kondé
Pycnonotus jocosus

HABITAT   : Commonly seen all over the island.

FOOD   : Omnivore. Eats fruits, seeds, insects.

REPRODUCTION : Three pinkish, spotted eggs laid in a small cup-shaped nest of thin grasses, fibres, etc., placed in trees, shrubs or bamboo hedges some 2 metres above ground. Hatching time about 15 days. Young stay a further fortnight in nest.

REMARKS   : One pair of birds escaping from a cage during the 1892 cyclone are said to be the ancestors of all the bulbuls on the island. Calls attractive. The bird is aggressive, and dangerous to other birds. Tends to be gregarious in winter. Female slightly smaller than male, has a slightly smaller red spot on the cheek and also a smaller crest. The bird is said to perform various tricks if trained. Easy to rear in captivity.

Order Passeriformes.   *Fam. Pycnonotidae.*

11. Ring-necked parakeet; Rose ringed parakeet *(Plate 13)*
Petite cato
Psittacula krameri

HABITAT	:	Locally common where grains, e.g. maize are abundant.
FOOD	:	Medium sized seeds, leaves and occasionally insects.
REPRODUCTION	:	Four to five white eggs laid in holes, e.g. of trees. Only the female sits on the eggs but is fed by the male . Hatching time about 23 days.
REMARKS	:	The bird is a pest and destroys grain. Is social, and attacks plants in groups. Escaped from a cage *c a* 1886.
		Must not be confused with the endemic parrot in which the female has a grey beak. In the introduced species both male and female have a pink beak.

Order Psittaciformes.   *Fam. Psittacidae.*

12. Rock dove
Colombe; Pigeon
Columba livia

HABITAT	:	Locally common in some areas, e.g. Port Louis market.
FOOD	:	Seeds and grains.
REPRODUCTION	:	Two white eggs laid in a rough nest of plant material, e.g. twigs. Hatching time 16 to 18 days. Young fed on a secretion of the stomach of the parents called pigeon milk.
REMARKS	:	Male and female alike in colouration. The species is an escape from domestication dating back to French times. Pigeons drink by keeping the beak in water and pumping up the liquid.

Order Columbiformes.   *Fam. Columbidae.*

13. Spice finch
Pingo; Damier
Lonchura punctulata

HABITAT   : Found in open country.

FOOD   : Small seeds and grains, e.g. those of grasses.

REPRODUCTION : Four to five white eggs laid in a rough nest placed high in vegetation. Nest has a lateral entrance.

REMARKS   : Call very low. Female paler than male. Flock with waxbills and fodies to feed on *Panicum*, etc. in the non-reproductive season. Young different in appearance from adult due to absence of spots.

Order Passeriformes.   *Fam Ploceidae.*

14. Spotted dove
Grosse tourterelle; Tourterelle à collier
Streptopelia chinensis

HABITAT : Occasional in open places where it is seen feeding on the ground.

FOOD : Seeds of various plants.

REPRODUCTION : Two white eggs laid in a perfunctory nest of twigs made in 4-5 days. Nest fairly low in vegetation. Hatching time about fifteen days. Young stay in nest for about eighteen days more. Has well marked courtship habits.

REMARKS : Probably introduced during French times.

Order Columbiformes.   Fam. Columbidae.

15. Waxbill *(Plate 15)*
Bengali
Estrilda astrild

HABITAT : Locally common in open country.

FOOD : Small seeds or grains, e.g. those of grasses.

REPRODUCTION : Four to six small white eggs laid in a large, domed nest with a lateral tubular entrance. Nest material partly woven. The nest is placed in vegetation, the male looking after the outside architecture and the female setting up the interior. Male slightly different from female. Both male and female sit on the eggs. Hatching time some twelve days, the young staying about a further fortnight in the nest.

REMARKS : Introduced from South Africa during the French period as a cage bird. Gathers in flocks with spice finches and cardinal birds to feed on *Panicum* and similar grasses during the non-reproductive season. A small, attractive, pink-billed bird often kept in cages.

Order Passeriformes.   *Fam. Estrildidae.*

16. Weaver bird; Village weaver *(Plate 16)*
Serin du Cap; Tisserin
Ploceus cucullatus

HABITAT   : Locally common in various areas.

FOOD   : Grains, seeds and insects.

REPRODUCTION : Eggs laid in a carefully woven nest of plant material like grass leaves. The nest, located at the extremity of palm leaves or of thin branches, has its entrance underneath. Nest made by male. Juvenile males sometimes start nests which they do not complete. Many nests are found on the same tree, hence the name republic bird.

REMARKS   : Both sexes similar outside the breeding season. During breeding male has a conspicuous yellow body with a black patch on the throat. The bird is a pest, eating cultivated seeds or grain.

Order Passeriformes.   *Fam. Ploceidae.*

17. Yellow fronted canary
Serin du pays
Serinus mozambicus

HABITAT : Seen mainly in some wooded areas like casuarina plantations near the seaside.

FOOD : Small seeds.

REPRODUCTION : Three to four bluish, slightly spotted eggs laid in a small, cup-shaped nest highly placed in vegetation. Hatching time 12 to 14 days. Young stay a further fortnight in nest.

REMARKS : In spite of the name *serin du pays*, the bird is an exotic. Was introduced from Tropical Africa as a cage bird in French times. Female duller than male.

Order Passeriformes.   Fam. Fringillidae.

D

MIGRANTS

There are a number of birds which reach our shores accidentally (driven by air currents or bad weather, for example) and others which visit us regularly coming here during our summer. They are mostly species which keep to the vicinity of water and the commonest are the following:

1. **Common sandpiper**
   Baise-roche; Guignette
   Actitis hypoleucos

   Recognised by the constant bobbing of head and tail. Small (about 20 cm long). Seen by the sea-side and inland near water. Often solitary. Looks like 2, 3 and 6 below.

2. **Curlew sandpiper**
   Bécasseau cocorli
   Calidris ferruginea

   Slightly downcurved black bill. Usually in flocks by the seaside and sometimes inland near water. Small (about 20 cm long). Looks like 1, 3 and 6. Some individuals stay here throughout the year but do not breed.

3. **Greater sand plover**
   Pluvier de Geoffroy
   Charadius leschenaulti

   Short black beak. White stripe above eye. Usually single by the seaside. Runs with a characteristic gait, head "pulled in". Looks like 1, 2, 6.

4. **Greenshank**
    Chevalier
    Tringa nebularia

    Thin, black, slightly upturned beak. Seen by the seaside and inland near water. Not very common.

5. **Grey plover**
    Pluvier suisse
    Pluvialis squatarola

    Short heavy beak. Large size (about 30 cm long). Usually single by the seaside.

6. **Sanderling**
    Calidris alba

    Short pointed beak. Always quickly on the move. Looks like 1, 2 and 3. Usually by the seaside. Not very common.

7. **Turnstone**
    Tourne-pierres
    Arenaria interpres

    Legs orange. The name is derived from the habit of turning over stones, etc. to find food. Seen by the seaside and inland near water. Some individuals stay throughout the year but do not breed here.

8. **Whimbrel**
    Petit corbigeau
    Numenius phaeopus

    Very long curved beak. Usually by the seaside. Some individuals stay throughout the year but do not breed here.

E

VISITORS

Our island is also graced by occasional or rare visits from a number of birds which have points of interest. For example, among land birds, the broad billed roller of Madagascar *(Eurystomus glaucurus)* impresses by its beauty and the cattle egret *(Bubulcus ibis)* is worth attention for its habit of perching on the back of large mammals to remove parasites.

The sea bird visitors are more numerous. The immaculate white tern *(Gygis alba)* has the ability to fly backwards while the lesser frigate *(Fregata ariel)* has an interesting courting habit. The male has, below the throat, a red pouch which it can inflate while courting the female in a striking display.

Size is evident in the giant petrel *(Macronectes giganteus)* and in the yellow-billed albatross *(Diomedea chlororhynchos)*. But the record breaker of all is a smaller bird, the pintado petrel or Cape pigeon *(Daption capense)*. A specimen was ringed on 27.6.57 at Cape Campbell in New Zealand. It was captured on 18.8.58 at Cap Malheureux in Mauritius and during its period of migration must have covered at least 10,000 kilometres.

INDEX